How many little letters can you find?

Answers: This page: 3; Title page: 6; By the pond: 4; At a party: 7; On the beach: 6; On safari: 7; In the woods: 6; At the lake: 6; In the classroom: 7; In the snow: 6; From the treehouse: 2; A stony slope: 6; Camping: 6; Blowing bubbles: 12.

From Me to You, Love God
Text © 2025 by Claire Freedman
Illustrations © 2025 by Emily Boughton

Published by Kregel Children's, an imprint of Kregel Publications, 2450 Oak Industrial Dr. NE, Grand Rapids, MI 49505. www.kregel.com. Original edition published by SPCK Publishing in English under the title *From Me to You, Love God*.

All rights reserved. No part of this book may be reproduced, stored in a retrieval system, or transmitted in any form or by any means—for example, electronic, mechanical, photocopy, recording, or otherwise—without the publisher's prior written permission or by license agreement. The only exception is brief quotations in printed reviews.

A catalog record for this book is available from the British Library.

ISBN 978-0-8254-4968-0

Printed in China
25 26 27 28 29 30 / 5 4 3 2 1

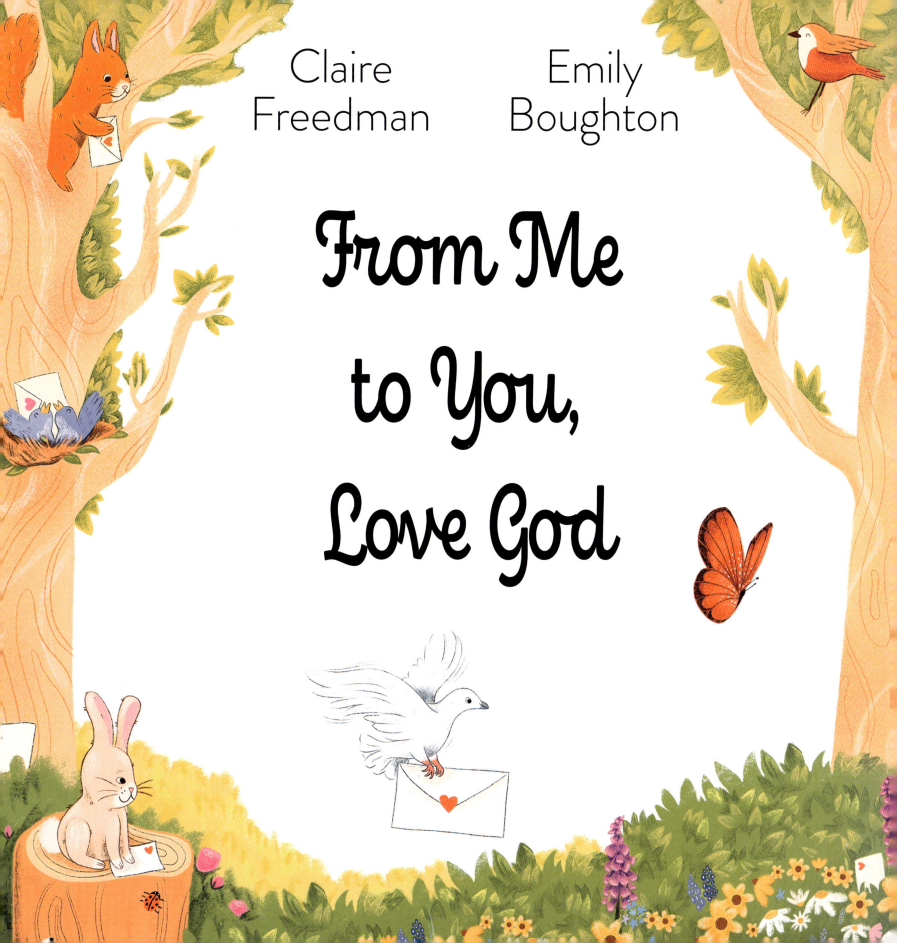

If God sent you a letter,
He'd say, "I love you so!
You're very precious to me,
and I want you to know."

God made you,
and He knows your name,
and so it's no surprise,
that the one and only,
uniquely YOU,
is perfect in His eyes!

God's love shines through your family,
their kindness, hugs, and care,

in fun and friends and holidays,
God's love is everywhere!

soft fluffy clouds, blue sunny skies,
and mountains oh so tall.

Life is a great adventure,
new paths you take each day.
It's good to have God's hand to hold
because He knows the way!

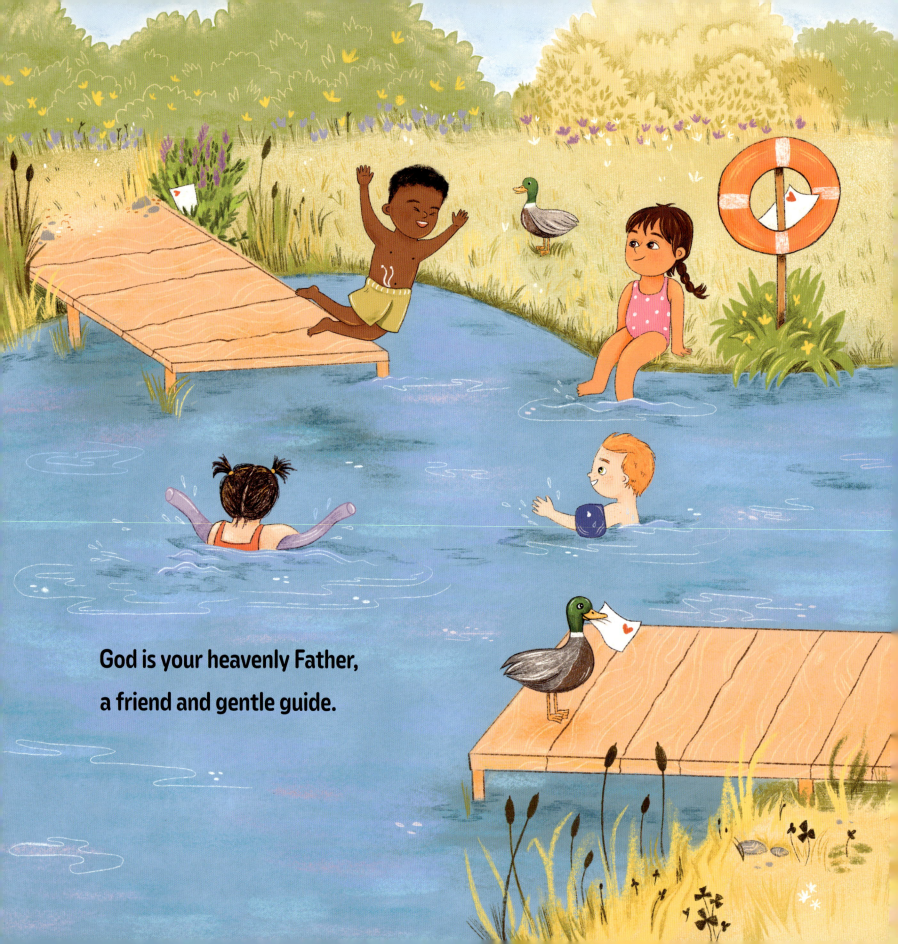

God is your heavenly Father,
a friend and gentle guide.

You never need to feel alone when God is by your side.

If you're naughty, God still loves you,
though He's pleased when you act good.

He'll help you do whatever's right—
those things you know you should.

God can see if you're happy,

He knows when you feel sad.

He loves you and He'll help you

through good times and the bad.

Tell Him all of your secrets,
your worries, and your fears.
God always has time to listen,
and He always, ALWAYS, cares.

But even if the road is hard,
like a steep and stony slope,

just like the rainbow after rain,
with God, there's always HOPE!

God loves you beyond the moon
that shimmers silvery bright.
He watches you snuggled in bed,
so you can sleep safely each night.

So now that you know God loves you,
share His news from east to west—
God's love is meant for EVERYONE.
His love is the very best!